# THE KEEPER OF SHEEP

# THE KEEPER OF SHEEP

*(O Guardador de Rebanhos)*

By

**Alberto Caeiro / Fernando Pessoa**

translated from the Portuguese
by Edwin Honig and Susan M. Brown

**The Sheep Meadow Press**
**Riverdale-on-Hudson, New York**

# ACKNOWLEDGMENTS

These translations are printed with the permission of Sra. D. Henriqueta Madalena Rosa Dias, the poet's sister, for the Estate of Fernando Pessoa.

New versions of poems II, IX, X, XIV, XXVIII, XXX, XXXII, XLIII, and XLVIII, which originally appeared in *Selected Poems by Fernando Pessoa,* translated by Edwin Honig, The Swallow Press, Chicago, 1971, appear here with the permission of Ohio University Press / Swallow Press.

Printed in the United States of America

All inquiries and permission requests should be addressed to the Publisher, The Sheep Meadow Press, P. O. Box 1345 Riverdale-on-Hudson, N.Y. 10471.

Typesetting by Keystrokes, Lenox, Massachusetts

Distributed by Persea Books
225 Lafayette Street
New York, N.Y. 10012

First Edition

Library of Congress Cataloging in Publication Data

Pessoa, Fernando, 1888-1935.
    The Keeper of sheep.

    Translation of: O guardador de rebanhos.
    I. Title.
PQ9261.P417G813 1986        869.1'41        85-31732
ISBN 0-935296-61-1 (pbk.)

# CONTENTS

# Introduction

The complete sequence of forty-nine poems that makes up *The Keeper of Sheep (O Guardador de Rebanhos)* is offered here for the first time in English translation. The work was produced by the fictitious shepherd and "master," Alberto Caeiro, a heteronym of the multiple poet Fernando Pessoa (1888–1935), sometimes called "the man who never was" and perhaps the most enigmatic of the notable poets writing in this century.

Often regarded as Portugal's best poet in four hundred years, Pessoa remains largely unknown to an international audience fifty years after his death, although several new translations in the major languages, appearing especially during the last decade, have begun to ameliorate the situation. His more than a thousand poems and essays, distributed among a handful of heteronyms, challenge even sympathetic readers of Portuguese and English, the languages he wrote in all his life. The bulk of his work published so far has become an object lesson in the effects of bilingualism and the use of multiple personae. His art might never have existed without the curious interfusion sustained between both languages and without the splitting and grafting of personality among the cast whose works and lives he invented. Alberto Caeiro was the central figure of the group he called his "coterie," and it was to Caeiro's vatic innocence and special authority that the others—Álvaro de Campos, Ricardo Reis, and Fernando Pessoa himself—seem to have deferred.

In the now famous letter to Adolfo Casais Monteiro, the literary critic, Pessoa explains the origin of Caeiro and the poems of *The Keeper of Sheep*, together with other developments concerning his advent.

One day—it was March 8, 1914—I went over to a high desk, and taking a piece of paper, began to write standing, as I always do when possible. And I wrote some thirty poems, one after another, in a sort of ecstasy, the nature of which I am unable to define. It was the triumphant day of my life, and never will there be another like it. I began with the title, 'O Guardador de Rebanhos.' What followed was the appearance of someone in me to whom I immediately gave the name Alberto Caeiro. Forgive the absurdity of the sentence: In me there appeared my master. That was my immediate reaction. So much so that, scarcely were those thirty-odd poems written when I took more paper and wrote, again without stopping, the six poems constituting 'Chuva Obliqua'/'Oblique Rain'/by Fernando Pessoa. Straight away and fully formed .... It was the return of Fernando Pessoa/Alberto Caeiro to Fernando Pessoa himself. Or, better, it was the reaction of Fernando Pessoa to his nonexistence as Alberto Caeiro. Once Alberto Caeiro had appeared, I instinctively and subconsciously tried to find disciples for him. Out of his false paganism I plucked the latent Ricardo Reis; I discovered the name and adapted it to him, because I had already *seen* him at that time. And suddenly, both stemming from and opposed to Ricardo Reis, there impetuously arose in me a new individual. At once and on the typewriter, without interruption or correction, there surged up the Triumphal Ode of Álvaro de Campos, the ode of that title along with the man of that name. Then I created a nonexistent coterie.... It's as if it all happened independently of me.

*The Keeper of Sheep* became the turning point of Pessoa's career and the psychogenetic model of poetic liberation. Caeiro's impact on Pessoa's development shows up, at one end, in the haunted urban poetry of Campos and, at the other, in the recessive classicism of the self-exiled Reis's poems. From early on, Pessoa juggled with the modes of all three heteronymic poets in one uneasy balance of consciousness. This tendency is still evident in the last poems of the *Cancioneiro,* that collection of lyrics he had been writing since 1902.

Pulsating through Pessoa's machinations with literary personality is an odd blending of patriotic feeling with a lifelong pursuit of the occult. Such preoccupations, if they did nothing else, bolstered Pessoa's self-perception as an emissary poet and "super-Camões": someone who might become the major force in heralding a new Golden Age of Portuguese poetry, its prime theoretician and practitioner— a kind of Portuguese Ezra Pound. Add to this his studious avoidance of any personal relationships that might distract him from his mission, and it grows clear why the price he had to pay was continual self-effacement, renunciation, isolation, and an unrelieved and deepening introversion. In the little that is known of his personal life, his pervasive monasticism is glimpsed through a typical sentence in his correspondence with Ophélia, an office girl he was trying not to fall in love with around 1920: "My destiny belongs to another law whose existence you do not even sense."

But even if his life was lived among the shadows, some of its crucial turns bear upon the evolution of his principled esthetic and the poetry that issued from it. Born in Lisbon on June 13, 1888, Pessoa was to find himself uprooted before he was eight years old from his country, his language, and a basic sense of family. His father, a self-educated music critic for a Lisbon daily, died of consumption in July 1893; a year and a half later his mother married, by proxy, João Miguel Rosa, the newly appointed Portuguese consul to South Africa, and Pessoa went to live with her and his stepfather in the sedate Victorian city of Durban.

Between 1896 and 1905, he attended English schools, quickly absorbing the English language and its literary traditions. He read closely Milton, Shakespeare, Pope, Byron, Shelley, Keats, Wordsworth, Tennyson, Poe, Carlyle, and Dickens. He went on subsequently to imitate the stylistic modes of such writers, even while Portuguese continued to be spoken at home. One critic has urged that since Pessoa's genius was generated in part by his ability to translate perceptions framed in the Victorian mold into his native language, he came to see how through the medium of English he might infuse Portuguese poetry with the bright newness and energy it seemed to lack.

At sixteen he won the Queen Victoria Memorial Prize for a literary essay at Durban High School. He had already been writing English poems—many of them published only recently—under the name of Alexander Search, an early experiment with persona. His need to embody dramatic voices who search out their identity through a series of poems later spurred Pessoa to embark upon his heteronymic adventure. His distinct voices, lyrically rendered from within a dramatic center, could all be controlled and conditioned by the impersonal stage-manager Fernando Pessoa himself.

Though his English poems smack more of the library than of the street, Pessoa's bilingualism was rich enough to feed many of his literary compositions, and of the three hundred poems published in his lifetime, short of a fifth were written in English and French. He translated freely from and into Portuguese, even to the point of producing a short mystery novel in English. His bent toward English might have made him a minor British poet (see *35 Sonnets, Epithalamium, Inscriptions, Antinous,* all published in Portugal between 1918 and 1921) had he gone, as the English poet Roy Campbell later did, from Durban to Oxford. Instead, he returned to Lisbon, and subsequently quit his studies at the university there. He tried to set himself up as a printer but failed, and by 1908 settled for a job as a commercial correspondent in French and English. Never to leave Lisbon again, he had clearly made up his mind by 1912 to become Portugal's leading literary figure.

That same year he launched his publishing career with two articles in the journal *A Águia*. In "The New Portuguese Poetry, Sociologically Considered" and "The New Portuguese Poetry, Psychologically Considered," Pessoa predicted that the poetry would inaugurate a new era of civilization, and somewhat less blatantly, announced himself as the successor to Camões, the nation's great sixteenth-century poet. The articles started him on a lifetime occupation of publishing his theories and opinions across a wide spectrum of cultural life, and demonstrate the writer's uncommon mixture of hard logic and mystical nationalistic thinking in his prose.

Even more significantly, Pessoa's literary journalism began to flesh out those problems he would have to cope with as a poet of high ambitions. A basic problem has to do with the inherent contradiction within the human spirit concerning its opposition to reality. Stated briefly and rather barely: the human spirit cannot accept dualistic thinking, since the idea of an absolute reality implies the notion of unity; and yet by its nature the human spirit must think dualistically, since it inevitably strives to see things externally as well as internally. This constant persuasion to think in terms of Unity and Oneness leads the Pantheist, for example, to see matter and spirit as real, while for the Transcendentalist they are an illusion. Pessoa, intent upon developing a system that would allow for paradox and embrace self-contradiction, called for a Transcendental Pantheism, based on relative truths, which makes room for a variety of points of view held simultaneously.

The problem of reality haunted him from the time of Alexander Search's early English poems and Pessoa's Portuguese poems written on his return to Lisbon. It centered upon the inquiring mind that keeps trying to pull back the veils of illusion in order to move beyond the appearance of things so as to perceive some operative truth for his poetry. Characteristically, this preoccupation with a single truth is what he vividly depicts, in English, as early as 1910:

> There is for me—there was—a wealth of meaning in a thing so ridiculous as a doorkey, a nail on a wall, a cat's whiskers. There is for me a fullness of spiritual suggestion in a fowl with its chickens strutting across the road. There is for me a meaning deeper than human fears in the smell of sandal-wood, in the old tins on a trash heap, in a matchbox lying in the gutter, in two dirty papers, which on a windy day will roll and chase each other down the street. For poetry is astonishment, admiration, as of a being fallen from the skies taking full consciousness of his fall, astonished about things. As of one who knew [what] things [were] in their souls, striving to remember this knowledge, remembering that it was not thus he knew them, not under these forms and these conditions, but remembering nothing more.

Pessoa kept shifting from one literary movement to another, testing its tenets in his writing and moving on. He experimented with Symbolism, Impressionism, and Futurism, but mainly with something called Intersectionism, a self-coined poetics based on an effort to express multiple sensations by forcing the reader to grasp simultaneously various realities which occur in different time-space dimensions. But gradually he came to focus on what he called Sensationism, a theory developed around the heteronymic explosion. Sensationism is an attitude "analogous to theosophy" that attempts "to be, not a religion, but the fundamental truth that underlies all religious systems alike." It must oppose any system that tries to exclude other systems. Writing in English, he endeavors to rationalize the process in personal terms:

> Having accustomed myself to have no beliefs and no opin-

ions, lest my aesthetic feeling should be weakened, I grew soon to have no personality at all except an expressive one. I grew to be a mere apt machine for the expression of moods which became so intense that they grew into personalities and made my very soul the mere shell of their casual appearance, even as theosophists say that the malice of nature-spirits sometimes makes them occupy the discarded astral corpses of men and frolic under the cover of their shadowy semblances [substances].

If Sensationism is the theory, the creation of personae is its poetic facilitation, and depersonalization, the method of expression. In 1914 Pessoa invented Alberto Caeiro, the embodiment of the liberating poetic consciousness, to initiate his heteronymic drama. But Pessoa's account of its origin, in the letter to Casais Monteiro quoted earlier, does not quite accurately represent the situation surrounding the event. For Caeiro, as we now know, had been "born" earlier, as the recent uncovering of manuscripts written prior to that famous date reveals. But because Pessoa wanted to create the myth of a spontaneous poet, he pretended that Caeiro occurred "all of a sudden." To highlight the quality of an eternal innocent, one whose wisdom flowed unself-consciously from the spirit, he wove the bucolic aspect into his fictional biography, making him a simple keeper of sheep, the type who is almost always at peace with himself and whose thoughts are contained and calm. Alberto Caeiro is reported to have been born in Lisbon in April 1889, and to have died of tuberculosis in 1915. Again the chronological detail is misleading, since Caeiro appears later as the author of another series of poems, "The Shepherd in Love" (*O Pastor Amoroso*), and of a number of uncollected poems, some dated as late as 1930. But Caeiro had taken up a fixed place as the antithesis to all Pessoa stood for, and in *The Keeper of Sheep* unraveled an argument refusing Pessoa's metaphysical notions and other futile concerns, which must be swept aside if the poet is to gain a secure foothold on modernist ground. *The Keeper of Sheep*, like *Song of Myself*, became a new poetic manifesto, proclaiming the unknowable and manifold nature of reality as something perceptible only to the unthinking and intensely receptive bodily senses, particularly the eye. Caeiro's persistent attacks on learning, Christianity, and rational thought are intended to strip away all preconceptions that prevent one from seeing things "as they are." Any thought system blinds one to the simple truth that all things have a natural existence in the present, and there is no other meaning than that to be deciphered from their appearance. Caeiro exists solely in what he sees, in the diversity of nature, and not in his mind reflecting the outer world. Learning, for him, is unlearning; feeling, not thinking; and being is a thoughtless flowing and merging with the world of the senses, its only reality. And, since the self is what vanishes in the process of self-discovery, the poetic urge becomes an empty stage for the convenience of invented characters, each of whom manufactures its own reality.

His creation of the shepherd poet not only led Pessoa to a principle of high poetic potentiality, allowing him to embark on his career as a multifaceted poet in the modern movement; it also brought him into the international arena at a time when the Portuguese language had no other literary figure capable of achieving comparable poetic mastery in modern terms. As his works become known, Pessoa may at last be seen as having brought into existence the precious means by which writers in Portuguese can assimilate his inventions, as liberating and challenging as those discovered by Rilke, Pound, and Valéry were for German, English, and French poets. In this way, "the man who never was" becomes not only the man who is, but also the man who will be.

*The Keeper of Sheep* derives from the Portuguese text of *O Guardador de Rebanhos* in the Nova Aguilar edition of *Obra Completa* by Fernando Pessoa, Rio de Janeiro, 1983. Since there exists no definitive scholarly edition of Pessoa's work in the Portuguese language, the translators have had to make specific determinations based on this and previous Aguilar editions, which often vary without editorial explanation.

We are grateful to Professors Alexandrino Severino, Janet W. Sullivan, and George Monteiro for pointed and often searching comments on developing versions of the translation. José Blanco of the Gulbenkian Foundation and Stanley Moss of The Sheep Meadow Press offered thoughtful suggestions in many instances, and the Poetry Society of America encouraged us by awarding this work its first translation prize in 1984.

Production of the manuscript was aided throughout by Dr. David Lloyd and Dr. Paul Acker, whose patience and skills helped us prepare successive drafts and the final copy for the printer.

E.H./S.M.B.

**THE KEEPER OF SHEEP**

## I. I never kept sheep

I never kept sheep,
But it's as if I'd done so.
My soul is like a shepherd.
It knows wind and sun
Walking hand in hand with the Seasons
Observing, and following along.
All of Nature's unpeopled peacefulness
Comes to sit alongside me.
Still I'm sad, as a sunset is
To the imagination,
When it grows cold at the end of the plain
And you feel the night come in
Like a butterfly through the window.

But my sadness is comforting
Because it's right and natural
And because it's what the soul should feel
When it already thinks it exists
And the hands pick flowers
And the soul takes no notice.

Like the clanking of cowbells
Beyond the bend in the road,
My thoughts are happy.
My only regret is knowing they're happy
Because if I didn't know it,
They'd be glad and happy
Instead of unhappy and glad.

Thinking is discomforting like walking in the rain
When the wind increases, making it look as if it's raining harder.

I've no ambitions or desires.
My being a poet isn't an ambition.
It's my way of being alone.

And if sometimes in my fancy
I desire to be a lamb
(Or the whole flock of sheep
So I can go all over the hillside
And be many happy things at the same time),
It's only because I feel what I'm writing when the sun sets
Or when a cloud's hand passes over the light
And a silence runs off through the grass.

When I sit down to write a poem
Or when ambling along the main roads and bypaths,
I write lines on the paper of my thoughts,
I feel the staff in my hands
And glimpse an outline of myself
On top of some low-lying hill,
Watching over my flock and seeing my ideas,
Or watching over my ideas and seeing my flock,
And smiling vaguely like one who doesn't understand what's said
And likes to pretend he does.

I greet everyone who'll read me,
Tipping my wide-brimmed hat to them
As they see me at my door
Just as the coach tips the top of the hill.
I salute them and wish them sunshine,
And rain when rain is called for,
And may their houses contain
Near an open window
Somebody's favorite chair
Where they sit, reading my poems.

4

And when reading my poems thinking
Of me as something quite natural—
An ancient tree, for instance,
In whose shade they thumped down
When they were children, tired after play,
Wiping the sweat off their hot foreheads
With the sleeve of their striped smocks.

**II.** My glance is clear like a sunflower

My glance is clear like a sunflower.
I usually take to the roads,
Looking to my right and to my left,
And now and then looking behind me....
And what I see each moment
Is that something I'd never seen before,
And I'm good at noticing such things....
I know how to feel the same essential wonder
That an infant feels if, on being born,
He could note he'd really been born....
I feel that I am being born each moment
Into the eternal newness of the World....

I believe in the World as in a daisy
Because I see it. But I don't think about it
Because thinking is not understanding....
The World was not made for us to think about
(To think is to be eye-sick)
But for us to look at and be in tune with....

I have no philosophy: I have senses....
If I speak of Nature, it's not because I know what Nature is,
But because I love it, and that's why I love it,
For a lover never knows what he loves,
Why he loves or what love is....

Loving is eternal innocence,
And the only innocence is not to think....

**III.** Leaning over the window sill at sunset

Leaning over the window sill at sunset
And, sidelong, knowing there are fields before me,
I read the book of Cesário Verde
Until my eyes burn.

How sorry I am for him! He was a man of the country
Who walked like a prisoner-at-large through the city.
But the way he looked at houses,
And his way of noticing streets,
And his way of taking things in,
Is the way of someone looking at trees,
Someone lowering his gaze to the road he follows,
Taking in the flowers in the fields....

This is why he had that enormous sadness
He never really said he felt,
But wandered through the city
Like someone ambling in the country
And sad as crushing flowers in a book
And sticking plants in a pot....

**IV.** This afternoon a thunderstorm broke

This afternoon a thunderstorm broke
Through the hillsides of the sky
Like a gigantic boulder....
Like someone shaking out a tablecloth
From a window high up,
And the crumbs coming down all at once
Making a racket as they fall,
So the rain poured from the sky
And darkened the roadways....

When bolts of lightning tore the air
And jolted space
Like a giant nay-saying head,
I don't know why—I wasn't afraid—
I began to pray to Saint Barbara
Like somebody's old aunt....

Ah! and my praying to Saint Barbara
Made me feel even simpler
Than I think I am....
I felt domesticated, a homebody,
Someone who'd passed his whole life
Peaceably, like the garden wall;
Having ideas and feelings in having them,
As a flower has fragrance and color....

I felt like one who could believe in Saint Barbara....
Ah, to be able to believe in Saint Barbara!

(Someone who believes in Saint Barbara,
Can he claim she's real and visible,
Or what can he claim about her?)

(What a lie! What do
Flowers, trees, and sheep know
Of Saint Barbara?....A tree limb,
If it thought, could never construe
Angels and saints.... Nor could it think the sun
Is God and the thunderstorm an angry mob overhead....
Ah, how sick, how stupid and mixed up
Are the simplest human beings
Next to trees and plants
In their sheer health and simplicity of being!)

And thinking all this,
I grew less happy once again....
I grew as dark and sick and sullen
As a day with its daylong threat of thunderstorm
That even at dusk hasn't yet arrived....

**V.** There's metaphysics enough in not thinking about anything

There's metaphysics enough in not thinking about anything.

What do I think of the World?
How do I know what I think of the World?
If I got sick I'd think about that.

What idea do I have of things?
What opinion do I have of cause and effect?
What thought have I given God and the soul
And the creation of the World?
I do not know. For me to think about this is to close my eyes
And not to think. It's closing the curtains
Of my window (but it doesn't have curtains).

The mystery of things? How should I know?
The only mystery is there being people who think about mystery.
If you stand in the sun and close your eyes,
You begin not to know what the sun is
And think many things full of heat.
But you open your eyes and see the sun,
And can no longer think of anything
Because sunlight is worth more than the thoughts
Of all the philosophers and all the poets.
Sunlight knows nothing of what it does
And therefore never goes wrong but is good and commonplace.

Metaphysics? What's the metaphysics of those trees?
Being green and leafy and having branches
And giving fruit in season, none of which makes us reflect
To ourselves, we who don't know how to notice such things.
But what better metaphysics than theirs,

Which is that of not knowing what they live for
Nor knowing they do not know it?

"The inner constitution of things...."
"The inner meaning of the Universe...."
All of it's false, all of it doesn't mean a thing.
Incredible that such things can be thought about.
It's like thinking of whys and wherefores
When morning daylight breaks and through the trees
A misty golden lustre forces the dark to vanish.

To think of the inner meaning of things
Is something added on, like thinking of your health
Or taking a cup to water fountains.

The only inner meaning of things
Is their not having any at all.

I don't beleve in God because I never saw him.
If he wanted me to believe in him,
He'd certainly come and speak with me,
Come in through my door
And tell me, *Here I am!*

(This may sound ridiculous to those
Who, not knowing what it means to look at things,
Cannot understand someone who speaks of things
In that way of speaking that the awareness of things teaches.)

But if God is the flowers and the trees
And the mountains and sun and the moonlight,
Then I believe in him,
Then I believe in him each and every moment,

And my entire life is one prayer and one Mass,
And, with eyes and ears, one communion.

But if God is the trees and the flowers
And the mountains, sun and the moonlight,
What do I call him God for?
I call him flowers, trees, mountains, sun and moonlight
Because if he created himself for me to see—
Sun, moonlight, flowers, trees, mountains—
If he appears to me as trees, mountains,
Moonlight, sun and flowers,
It's because he wants me to know him
As trees, mountains, flowers, moonlight and sun.

And for this I obey him
(What more do I know of God than God knows of himself?),
I obey him by living spontaneously,
Like someone who opens both eyes and sees,
And I call him moonlight, sun, flowers, trees, and mountains,
And I love him without thinking about him,
And I think of him, seeing and listening,
And I'm at his side each and every moment.

**VI.** To think of God is to disobey God

To think of God is to disobey God
Because God wanted us not to know him,
And therefore did not show himself to us....

Let's be calm and simple,
Like brooks and trees,
And God will love us for it, make us
Beautiful as brooks and trees,
And will give us the green of his spring,
And a river to go to when we are done!...

**VII.** From my village I see as much of the earth as can be
   seen in the Universe

From my village I see as much of the earth as can be seen
   in the Universe. . . .
That's why my village is as big as any other place on earth.
Because I am the size of what I see
And not the measure of my height. . . .

In the cities life is smaller
Than it is here in my house on top of this hill.
In the city big houses shut in sight under lock and key,
They blot out the horizon, they push our seeing down
   far out of range of the sky,
They shrink us because they take away what our seeing can
   offer us,
And they make us poor because our only wealth is seeing.

14

**VIII.** Once at mid-day in late spring

Once at mid-day in late spring
A dream came to me like a photograph.
I saw Jesus Christ come down to earth.
He came down the slope of a mountain,
Turned once more into a child,
Running and romping through the grass
And pulling up flowers to throw them away
And laughing so loud he was heard far away.

He had escaped from the sky.
He was too much like us to pretend
He was the second person of the Trinity.
It was all false in the sky, all out of keeping
With the flowers and trees and rocks.
In the sky he always had to be serious
And now and then he had to become man again
And mount the cross and always be dying
With a crown of thorns all around his head
And the head of a spike hammered into his feet,
And even a rag around his waist
Like the black men in the picture books.
They didn't even let him have a father and mother
Like the other children.
His father was two people—
An old man named Joseph, who was a carpenter,
And wasn't his father;
And the other father a stupid dove,
The only ugly dove in the world
Because it wasn't from the world and wasn't a dove.
And his mother hadn't loved anyone before having him.

She wasn't a woman: she was a suitcase

In which he'd come out of the sky.
And they wanted him, who was born only of a mother,
And never had a father to love with respect,
To teach goodness and justice!

One day when God was sleeping
And the Holy Ghost was flying around,
He went to the chest of miracles and stole three.
With the first he made it impossible for anybody to know
    he'd escaped.
With the second he created himself eternally human
    and a child.
With the third he created a Christ eternally stuck to the cross
And left him nailed to the cross in the sky
And it serves as a model for the others.

Afterward he went off to the sun
And came down on the first light beam he could catch.
Today he lives with me in my village.
And he's a natural child with a wonderful laugh.
He wipes his nose on his right arm,
He splashes around in the puddles,
He picks flowers and loves them and forgets them.
He throws stones at the donkeys,
He steals fruit from the orchards
And runs away from the dogs, screaming and yelling.
And, because he knows they don't like it
And that everybody finds it funny,
He runs after the girls
Who stroll in groups along the roads
Carrying water jars on their heads,
And he lifts up their skirts.

He taught me everything.

He taught me to look at things.
He points out everything there is inside flowers.
He shows me how funny rocks are
When people take them in hand
And look slowly at them.

He speaks very badly of God to me.
He says he's a stupid sick old man,
Always spitting on the floor
And saying indecent things.
The Virgin Mary spends afternoons in eternity knitting
    stockings.
And the Holy Ghost scratches itself with its beak
And perches in chairs and dirties them up.
Everything in the sky is stupid like the Catholic Church.
And he tells me God doesn't understand a thing
About the things he's created—
"If it's he who created them, which I doubt.
He says, for instance, that the creatures sing his glory,
But the creatures don't sing anything.
If they sang they'd be singers.
The creatures exist, and nothing more,
And that's why they're called creatures."
And afterward, tired of speaking ill of God,
The Child Jesus falls asleep in my arms
And I carry him home against my breast.

+

He lives with me in my house halfway up the hill.
He's the Eternal Child, the God that was missing.
He's the human being that's natural,
He's the divine being that smiles and plays.
And that's how I know for certain
That he's really the Child Jesus.

And the child who's so human he's divine
Is this, my daily life as a poet,
And it's because he's always with me that I'm always a poet,
And that the slightest glance
Fills me with feeling,
And the tiniest sound, whatever it may be,
Seems to speak to me.

The New Child who lives where I live
Gives me one hand
And the other to all that exists,
And so we go along, the three of us, on whatever road's ahead,
Jumping and singing and laughing
And enjoying our common secret
Which is knowing through and through
There is no mystery in the world
And that all things are worth our while.

The Eternal Child is with me always.
My glance takes the direction of his pointing finger.
My hearing, happily alert to every sound,
Is his playful tickling in my ears.

We get along so well together
In the company of every thing
We never think of one another,
But live together, the two of us,
With an intimate understanding
Like the right hand with the left.

At nightfall we play jacks
On the doorstep of the house,
Serious, as befits a god and a poet,
And as if each jack

Were an entire universe
And would be enormously dangerous therefore
To let it fall to the ground.

Later I tell him stories about the doings of mankind
And he smiles because it's all so incredible.
He laughs at kings and those who aren't kings,
And it hurts him to hear me speak of wars,
And of commerce, and the navies
That are left as smoke in air on the high seas.
Because he knows it all lacks that truth
A flower has in bloom
Which moves with the light of the sun
Changing mountains and valleys
And making eyes ache at whitewashed walls.

Later he falls asleep and I put him to bed.
I carry him at my breast into the house
And lay him down, undress him slowly,
Like following a ritual, utterly clean and maternal,
Until he is all naked.

He sleeps within my soul
And sometimes wakes at night
And plays with my dreams.
He throws some upside down in the air,
He places some on top of others
And claps his hands alone,
Smiling at my sleep.

+

When I die, my little son,
Let me be the child, the smallest one.
Take me in your arms
And carry me inside your house.

Undress my tired human frame
And lay me in your bed.
Tell me stories if I waken
So I can fall asleep again.
And give me your dreams to play with
Until whatever day is born,
A day—and you know which.
+
This is the story of my Child Jesus.
For what conceivable reason
Should it be any less true
Than all that philosophers think of
And all that religions teach?

**IX.** I'm a keeper of sheep

I'm a keeper of sheep.
The sheep are my thoughts
And my thoughts are all sensations.
I think with my eyes and ears
And with my hands and feet
And with my nose and mouth.

To think a flower is to see it and smell it
And to eat a fruit is to taste its meaning.

That's why on a hot day
When I ache from enjoying it so much,
And stretch out on the grass,
Closing my warm eyes,
I feel my whole body lying full length in reality,
I know the truth and I'm happy.

**X.** "Hello there, keeper of sheep"

"Hello there, keeper of sheep,
You there, by the roadside,
What does the passing wind tell you?"

"That it's the wind and it passes,
That it's done so before,
And that it'll do so again.
And what does it tell you?"

"A good deal more than that.
It speaks to me of many other things.
Of memories and yearnings
And things that never were."

"You've never listened to the wind.
The wind speaks only of the wind.
What you heard it say was a lie,
And that lie is part of you."

**XI.** The woman over there has a piano

The woman over there has a piano
That's pleasant but it isn't the running of rivers
Or the murmuring trees make....

What should one have a piano for?
Better to have ears
And love Nature.

**XII.** The shepherds in Virgil played flutes and other things

The shepherds in Virgil played flutes and other things
And sang of love in a literary way.
(But then—I never read Virgil.
What should I read him for?)

But the shepherds in Virgil—poor things—are Virgil,
And Nature is ancient and beautiful.

**XIII.** Lightly, lightly, ever so lightly

Lightly, lightly, ever so lightly,
A wind passes so lightly,
And dies away, ever ever so lightly.
And I know not what I think
Nor do I try to know.

**XIV.** Rhymes mean nothing to me. Only rarely

Rhymes mean nothing to me. Only rarely
Are two trees identical, standing side by side.
My thinking and writing are like flowers having color
But the way I express myself is less perfect
Because I lack the divine simplicity
Of being only what I appear to be.

I look and I am moved,
Moved as water flows when the ground slopes,
And my poetry is natural, like the rising of the wind....

**XV.** The four songs that follow now

The four songs that follow now
Are separate from anything I think,
They give the lie to everything I feel,
They are the opposite of all I am. . . .

I wrote them when I was ill
And that's why they're natural,
In keeping with what I feel.
They agree with what they disagree. . . .
When I'm sick I must think the opposite
Of what I think when I am well.
(Otherwise I wouldn't be sick.)
I must feel the opposite of what I feel
When I am well,
I must give the lie to my nature
As a being who feels in a certain way. . . .
I must be sick completely—ideas and everything.
When I'm sick, I'm not sick for any other reason.

That's why these songs that deny me
Have no power to deny me
And are the landscape of my soul at night,
The same one but its opposite. . . .

**XVI.** I'd give anything if only my life were an oxcart

I'd give anything if only my life were an oxcart
Squeaking down the road, early one morning
And later returning to where it started,
Toward nightfall, down the same road.

I'd have no need of hopes—I'd need only wheels...
As I grew old I'd have no wrinkles or white hair...
When I'd be of no further use, they'd pull off my wheels
And I'd lie there overturned and broken, at the bottom
   of a pit.

**XVII.** Such a potpourri of Nature on my plate

Such a potpourri of Nature on my plate!
Sisters of mine, these plants,
Companions of the fountains, saints
That no one prays to...

And they come cut up to our table
And in the hotels the noisy guests
Arrive with their strapped up bundles
And ask for "Salad," thinking nothing of it....
Thoughtlessly they ask Mother Earth
For her freshness and first children,
The first green words she utters,
The first things live and radiant
That Noah saw
When the flood subsided and the mountaintops
Green and soaking wet emerged
And in the sky where the dove appeared
The rainbow slowly faded....

**XVIII.** I'd give anything just to be the roadside dust

I'd give anything just to be the roadside dust
And the feet of the poor would trample me...

I'd give anything just to be the flowing rivers
And have the washerwomen at my banks...

I'd give anything to be the poplars along the river
And have just sky above and water down below...

I'd give anything to be the miller's mule
And have him beat me and value me...

O to be any of these rather than go through life
Looking behind and feeling sorrow....

**XIX.** The moonlight when it beats the grass

The moonlight when it beats the grass—
I'm not sure what it reminds me of....
I remember an old servant's voice
Telling me fairy tales.
And how Our Lady in beggar's clothes
Walked the roads at night
Bringing comfort to punished children....

If I can no longer believe such things are true
Why does moonlight beat the grass?

**XX.** The Tagus is lovelier than the river running through
  my village

The Tagus is lovelier than the river running through
  my village,
But the Tagus is not lovelier than the river running through
  my village
Because the Tagus isn't the river running through my village.
The Tagus has great steamships
And on it still bears—
For those who see in everything what's not there—
Some memory of the frigates.

The Tagus comes down from Spain
And in Portugal enters the sea.
Everyone knows this.
But few know which the river in my village is
And where it goes
And where it comes from.
That's why, since it involves fewer people,
The river in my village is freer and greater.

The Tagus takes you out into the World.
Beyond the Tagus there's America
And the fortune awaiting those who find it.
No one's ever wondered what lies beyond
The river of my village.

The river of my village makes no one think of anything.
Anyone standing alongside it is just standing alongside it.

**XXI.** If I could take a bite of the whole earth

If I could take a bite of the whole earth
And get a taste of it,
I'd be happier for a moment....
But I don't always want to be happy.
One must be unhappy now and then
Just to be able to be natural....

Not every day is fair,
And when there's a drought, you look for rain.
That's why I take the happy with the sad
Naturally, like someone not surprised
There are mountains and plains,
Rocks and grass....

One must be natural and easy,
Take the happy with the sad,
Feel as one who looks,
Think as one who walks,
And, when it's time to die, remember the day dies too,
And the sunset is beautiful, and beautiful too the enduring
    night....
That's how it is, and so be it....

**XXII.** Like someone opening his house door on a Summer's day

Like someone opening his house door on a Summer's day
And taking the heat of the fields full in the face,
Sometimes I'm suddenly hit smack in the face by Nature,
In the face of my senses,
And I get confused, disturbed, wanting to understand—
I'm not sure how or what. . . .

But who ordered me to want to understand?
Who told me I had to understand?

When Summer moves across my face
The delicate warm hand of its breeze,
I need only feel glad because it's breeze,
Or not so glad because it's heat,
And however I feel it,
So, since that's what I feel, it's my duty to feel it. . . .

**XXIII.** Like the sky, my blue gaze

Like the sky, my blue gaze
Is calm as water in sunlight.
That's what it is, blue and calm,
Because nothing startles it or gives it pause...

If I were to question and be startled,
New flowers would fail to be born in the fields
Nor would anything change in the sun to make it
    more beautiful....
(Even if new flowers were born in the fields
And the sun grew more beautiful,
I'd sense fewer flowers in the fields
And find the sun grown more ugly....
Because everything is as it is, and so is what it is,
And this I accept, and don't even feel grateful,
So as not to seem as if I were thinking all this....)

**XXIV.** What we see of things are those things

What we see of things are those things.
Why would we see one thing if there were another?
Why would seeing and hearing exist to deceive us
If seeing and hearing are seeing and hearing?

The main thing is knowing how to see,
Knowing how to see without thinking,
Knowing how to see when one sees,
And not thinking when one sees
Nor seeing when one's thinking.

But all this (what a shame we all wear a dressed-up soul!)—
All this demands serious looking into,
A thorough learning in how to unlearn
And a curtailing of freedom in that convent
Where poets say stars are eternal nuns
And flowers are pious penitents of a single day,
But where stars finally are nothing if not stars
And flowers nothing if not flowers,
Which is just why we call them stars and flowers.

**XXV.** The soap bubbles this child

The soap bubbles this child
Has fun blowing from a little reed
Are translucently a complete philosophy.
Clear, useless, and transient as Nature itself,
Companions to the eye, as things are,
They're what they are
In their airy, round precision,
And nobody, not even the child who lets them out,
Pretends they're more than they seem to be.

Some are hardly visible in the bright air.
They're like the passing breeze barely touching the flowers,
And we know it's passing
Only because something grows lighter within us,
Accepting everything more distinctly.

**XXVI.** Some days, when the light is perfect and precise

Some days, when the light is perfect and precise,
When things contain all the reality they can ever have,
I slowly ask myself why
I even attribute
Beauty to things.

Is there really beauty in a flower?
Is there really beauty in a fruit?
No, they've got color and form,
And existence—nothing else.
Beauty is the name for something that doesn't exist,
A name I give things for the pleasure they give me.
It means nothing.
Then why do I say of things, they're beautiful?

Yes, even I, who live only by living,
Am reached invisibly by men's lies
Before the things themselves,
Before the things that simply exist.

How hard to be oneself and see only the visible!

**XXVII.** Only Nature is divine, and she's not divine

Only Nature is divine, and she's not divine...

If I speak of her as a being
It's because to speak of her I must use the language of men,
Which endows things with personality,
And forces names upon things.
But things have neither name nor personality—
They exist, and the sky is vast and the earth wide,
And our hearts the size of a clenched fist....

Bless me for all I do not know.
I enjoy it all as one who knows there is always sun.

**XXVIII.** Today I read nearly two pages

Today I read nearly two pages
In a book by a mystic poet,
And I laughed like someone who'd been weeping and weeping.

Mystic poets are sick philosophers,
And philosophers are madmen.

Because mystic poets say that flowers feel
And say that stones have souls
And rivers have ecstasies in moonlight.

But flowers wouldn't be flowers if they felt anything—
They'd be people;
And if stones had souls they'd be living things, not stones;
And if rivers had ecstasies in moonlight,
They'd be sick people.

Only if you don't know what flowers, stones, and rivers are
Can you talk about their feelings.
To talk about the soul of flowers, stones, and rivers,
Is to talk about yourself, about your delusions.
Thank God stones are just stones,
And rivers nothing but rivers,
And flowers just flowers.

As for myself, I write out the prose of my poems
And I am satisfied,
Because I know all I can understand is Nature from the outside;
I don't understand it from inside
Because Nature hasn't any inside;
It wouldn't be Nature otherwise.

**XXIX.** I'm not always the same in what I say and write

I'm not always the same in what I say and write.
I change, but don't change much.
The color of flowers in sunlight isn't the same
As when a cloud goes by
Or when night sets in
And flowers are the color of the shadow.

But who looks closely sees they're the same flowers.
And so when I seem not to be agreeing with myself,
Pay close attention to me:
If I was turned to the right,
Now I've turned to the left,
But I'm always me, standing on both feet—
Always the same, thanks to earth and sky,
To my eyes and ears cocked,
And to the clear simplicity of my soul...

**XXX.** If they want me to be a mystic, fine. I'm a mystic

If they want me to be a mystic, fine. I'm a mystic.
I'm a mystic, but only of the body.
My soul is simple and doesn't think.

My mysticism is not wanting to know.
It's living without thinking about it.

I don't know what Nature is: I sing it.
I live on a hilltop
In a solitary whitewashed cabin.
And that's my definition.

**XXXI.** If at times I say that flowers smile

If at times I say that flowers smile
And if I should say that rivers sing,
It's not because I think there are smiles in flowers
And songs in rivers' running....
It's because that way I make deluded men better sense
The truly real existence of flowers and rivers.

Because I write for them to read me I sacrifice myself at times
To their stupidity of feeling....
I don't agree with myself yet I forgive myself
Because I'm solely that serious thing—an interpreter of Nature—
Because there are men who don't understand its language,
Being no language at all.

**XXXII.** Yesterday afternoon a city man

Yesterday afternoon a city man
Was talking at the door of the inn.
He was talking to me too.
He spoke of justice and the struggle to achieve justice
And of the suffering workers
And of ceaseless toil and hungry people
And of the rich, who just turn their backs to it all.

And, looking at me, he saw tears in my eyes
And smiled with satisfaction, thinking I felt
The hatred he did, and the compassion
He said he felt.

(But I was scarcely listening.
What does mankind matter to me
And what they suffer or think they suffer?
Let them be like me—they won't suffer.
All the world's troubles come from poking our noses in
   one another's business,
Whether to do good or to do bad.
Our soul, the sky, the earth, are all we need.
To want more is to lose it all and be unhappy.)

What I was thinking about
While the friend of mankind was talking
(And that's what moved me to tears)
Was how the distant tinkle of cowbells
As night came on
Was *nothing at all* like the sound of bells in a small chapel
Where flowers and brooks would go to Mass
Along with simple souls like mine.

(Thank God I'm not good,
And have the natural egoism of flowers
And of rivers following their course
Intent, without knowing it,
Only on flowering and flowing.
We've only one mission in the World:
That's to exist clearly
And know how to, without thinking about it.)

And the man had fallen silent, watching the sunset.
But what's a man who hates and loves got to do with the sunset?

**XXXIII.** Poor flowers in beds in neatly trimmed gardens

Poor flowers in beds in neatly trimmed gardens.
They seem to be afraid of the police....
But they're so good they bloom in the same way
And have the same ancient smile
They had for the first glance of the first man
Who saw them appear and touched them lightly
To see if they would speak...

**XXXIV.** I find it so natural not to think

I find it so natural not to think
That I start laughing sometimes when alone
At what, I really don't know, but something
Having to do with people who think....

What's my wall going to think of my shadow?
I ask myself sometimes till I'm aware
Of myself asking myself things....
And then don't like it and get annoyed,
As if I'd caught myself with my foot asleep....

What's this thing going to think of that one?
Nothing thinks anything.
Is the Earth aware of the stones and plants it contains?
If so, let her be....
What does this have to do with me?
If I thought of such things,
I'd stop seeing the trees and the plants
And I'd stop seeing the Earth,
Only to see my own thoughts....
I'd grow unhappy and stay in the dark.
And so, without thinking, I have the Earth and the Sky.

**XXXV.** The moonlight behind the tall branches

The moonlight behind the tall branches
The poets all say is more
Than the moonlight behind the tall branches.

But for me, who do not know what I think,—
What the moonlight behind the tall branches
Is, beyond its being
The moonlight behind the tall branches,
Is its not being more
Than the moonlight behind the tall branches.

**XXXVI.** And there are poets who are artists

And there are poets who are artists
And work on their poems
Like a carpenter on his planks! . . .

How sad, not knowing how to bloom!
Having to pile line upon line like someone building a wall
And looking to see if it fits, and removing it if it doesn't! . . .
When the only house of art is the whole Earth,
Which changes and is always good and always the same.

I think about this, not as one who thinks but as one who breathes,
And I watch the flowers and smile. . .
I don't know if they understand me
Or if I understand them,
But I know the truth is in them and in me
And in the divinity we share
By letting ourselves go and live with the Earth
And be borne on the breast of the satisfied Seasons
And letting the wind sing us softly to sleep
And having no dreams at all in our sleep.

**XXXVII.** Like a great blotch of filthy fire

Like a great blotch of filthy fire
The sunken sun stalls among remnant clouds.
From afar a vague whistle comes through the calmest afternoon.
It must be a train in the distance.

At the same moment a sense of indefinite yearning arrives
With some vague and mild desire
Appearing and disappearing.

Also, on the surface of streams
Occasional bubbles of water form,
Are born and dissolve,
And they have no meaning at all
Beyond being bubbles of water
That are born and dissolve.

**XXXVIII.** Blessed be the selfsame sun in other lands

Blessed be the selfsame sun in other lands
Making all men kin,
Since all men once a day gaze upon it, as I do,
And, at that pure moment,
Sensitive and cleansed,
Tearfully return
With a sigh scarcely felt
For man, primitive and true,
That saw the Sun rise and didn't yet worship it.
Because all this is natural—more natural
Than worshipping gold and God,
Art and morality...

**XXXIX.** The mystery of things, where is it

The mystery of things, where is it?
Where is that which never appears
To show us, at least, it's a mystery?
What's the river know about it and what, the tree?
And I, being no more than they, what do I know about it?
Whenever I look at things and think what men think of them,
I laugh like a brook freshly sounding off a rock.

Because the only hidden meaning of things
Is that they have no hidden meaning at all.
This is stranger than all the strangenesses,
And the dreams of all the poets,
And the thoughts of all the philosophers—
That things really are what they appear to be
And that there is nothing to understand.

Yes, here's what my senses learned all by themselves:
Things have no meaning—they have existence.
Things are the only hidden meaning of things.

**XL.** A butterfly passes before me

A butterfly passes before me
And for the first time in the Universe I note
That butterflies have neither motion nor color,
Just as flowers have neither fragrance nor color.
Color is what in the butterfly's wings has color,
In the butterfly's motion it's motion that moves,
Perfume is what has perfume in the perfume of the flower.
The butterfly is only a butterfly,
The flower only a flower.

**XLI.** At times, in the late afternoons of Summer

At times, in the later afternoons of Summer,
Though no breeze is stirring at all, it seems
For a moment a slight breeze goes by...
But the trees remain motionless
In every leaf of their leaves
And our senses had an illusion,
The illusion of something that would please them....

Oh, the senses—the sicklies who see and hear!
Were we as we should be
There'd be no need in us for illusion....
It would be enough to feel—distinct and energetic—
And not be concerned with what the senses are for...

But thank God for imperfection in the World
Because imperfection is a thing,
And having people who make mistakes is original,
And having sick people makes the World amusing.
Were there no imperfection, there'd be one thing less,
And there have to be many things
So that we've much to see and hear....

**XLII.** A coach passed down the road and went off

A coach passed down the road and went off;
And the road was neither more beautiful nor more drab.
Throughout the world human action is like that.
We neither remove nor add a thing: we pass by and forget;
And the sun is punctual, always, each and every day.

**XLIII.** Rather the flight of the bird passing and leaving no trace

Rather the flight of the bird passing and leaving no trace
Than creatures passing, leaving tracks on the ground.
The bird goes by and forgets, which is as it should be.
The creature, no longer there, and so, perfectly useless,
Shows it was there—also perfectly useless.

Remembering betrays Nature,
Because yesterday's Nature is not Nature.
What's past is nothing and remembering is not seeing.

Fly, bird, fly away; teach me to disappear!

**XLIV.** At night I suddenly waken

At night I suddenly waken,
And my watch fills the night completely.
I don't sense Nature outdoors.
My room is a something dark with vaguely white walls.
Outside there's repose, as though nothing existed.
Only the watch with its noise keeps going.
And this tiny thing full of complex gears on top of my table
Suffocates all existence on earth and above....
I'm about to lose myself thinking of what all this means,
But I stop, and in the night feel a smile creep to the corners
   of my mouth,
Because the only thing my watch symbolizes or means,
Filling the huge night with its tininess,
Is the curious sensation of filling the huge night
With its tininess....

**XLV.** There, way over there by the hillside, a row of trees

There, way over there by the hillside, a row of trees.
But what's a row of trees? Only trees.
Row and plural trees aren't things, they're names.

Poor human beings, always putting things in order,
Tracing lines from this thing to that thing,
Sticking labels with names on totally real trees,
And plotting parallels for latitude and longitude
On the innocent earth itself, so flourishing and much
    greener than that!

**XLVI.** One way or another

One way or another,
The moment permitting,
Able to say what I think at times,
And otherwise saying it poorly and jumbled,
I keep writing my poems without wanting to,
As if writing weren't something made up of gestures,
As if writing were something that happened to me
Like the sun outside shining on me.

I try saying what I feel
Without thinking about what I feel.
I try fitting words to the idea
Without going down a corridor
Of thought to find words.

I don't always succeed in feeling what I know I should feel.
My thought swims the river only quite slowly,
Heavily burdened by clothes men have made it wear.

I try divesting myself of what I've learned,
I try forgetting the mode of remembering they taught me,
And scrape off the ink they used to paint my senses,
Unpacking my true emotions,
Unwrapping myself, and being myself, not Alberto Caeiro,
But a human animal that Nature produced.

So I write, wanting to feel Nature, not even like a man,
But one who feels Nature, nothing more.
So I write, often well, often not,
Now hitting the nail on the head, and now not,
Falling down here, picking myself up there,
Yet always going ahead on my own like a pigheaded blind man.

Even so, I'm somebody
I'm the Discoverer of Nature.
I'm the Argonaut of true sensations.
I bring a new Universe into the Universe
Because I bring to the Universe its very own self.

This I feel, and this I write,
Knowing perfectly and not without seeing
That it's five o'clock in the morning
And the sun, though still not showing its head
Over the wall of the horizon,
May already be seen with its fingertips
Clawing the top of the wall
Of the horizon, full of low-lying hills.

## XLVII. On a terribly clear day

On a terribly clear day,
A day that made you wish you'd worked very hard
So you'd not work at all that day,
I caught a glimpse, like a road through the trees,
Of what might after all be the Big Secret,
That Great Mystery crooked poets talk about.

I saw that there is no Nature,
That Nature does not exist,
That there are mountains, valleys, plains,
That there are trees, flowers, grasses,
That there are rivers and stones,
But that there's no one great All these things belong to,
That any really authentic unity
Is a sickness of all our ideas.

Nature is simply parts, nothing whole.
Maybe this is the mystery they talk about.

And this, without stopping, without thinking,
Is just what I hit on as being the truth
That everyone goes around looking for in vain,
And that only I, because I wasn't looking for it, found.

**XLVIII.** From the highest window of my house

From the highest window of my house
With a white handkerchief I bid good-bye
To my poems going off to humanity.

And I'm neither happy nor sad.
That's the destiny of my poems.
I wrote them and must show them to everyone
Because I cannot do otherwise,
As the flower can't hide its color,
Or the river hide its flowing,
Or the tree its fruit-giving.

There they go off in the distance, as in a coach,
And I feel sorrow without wanting to,
Like bodily pain.

Who knows who's going to read them?
Who knows what hands they'll reach?

Flower, it was for eyes that my destiny picked me.
Tree, it was for mouths my fruit was plucked.
River, it was the destiny of my waters not to remain in me.
I yield, and feel almost happy,
Almost happy, like one who's tired of being sad.

Go, go from me!
The tree goes by, its remains strewn everywhere by Nature.
The flower wilts, its dust remains forever.
The river flows, entering the sea, and in its waters
    always its own remains.

Like the Universe, I pass and I remain.

**XLIX.** I go indoors, and shut the window

I go indoors, and shut the window.
They bring the lamp and say good night.
And my voice, content, says good night.
Oh, that my life were like this always:
The day full of sun, or gentle with rain,
Or in fury raging as if the World would end,
A soft afternoon with clusters of people going by,
Looked at with interest from the window,
The last friendly gaze turned to the repose of the trees,
And then, the window closed, the lamp lit,
Without reading a word, without thinking a thought or sleeping,
Feeling life flow through me like a river in its bed,
And there, outside, a vast silence like a god asleep.